WHO AM I?

Who am I?

Titles in the series

I am pink and curly-tailed, fat and grunting.
I live on a farm.

WHO AM I?

By Moira Butterfield
Illustrated by Wayne Ford

Thameside Press

Distributed in the United States by
Smart Apple Media
1980 Lookout Drive
North Mankato, MN 56003

Printed in Hong Kong

   Library of Congress Cataloging-in-Publication Data
Butterfield, Moira, 1961-
  Pig / Moira Butterfield.
    p. cm. — (Who am I?)
  Summary: Describes parts of a well-known animal and invites
the reader to identify it.
  ISBN 1-929298-91-9
  1. Landrace swine—Juvenile literature. 2. Swine—Juvenile
literature. [1. Pigs.] I. Title.

SF393.L3 B87 2000
636.4—dc21   00-022753

9 8 7 6 5 4 3 2 1

Editor: Stephanie Turnbull
Designer: Helen James
Illustrator: Wayne Ford / Wildlife Art Agency
Consultant: Jock Boyd

I'm very fat.
I grunt and squeal.
I'm always looking for a meal.
I like to wallow in a pool.
The muddy water keeps me cool.

Who am I?

Here is my eye.

I live on a farm with lots of other animals. The farmer looks after me, giving me food and water.

I lie in my hut and watch other animals in the field. Can you see a hare, a blackbird and a butterfly?

Here is my nose.

It is called a snout.
I use it to snuffle for
food on the ground.
The farmer has left
some special goodies
for me to find.

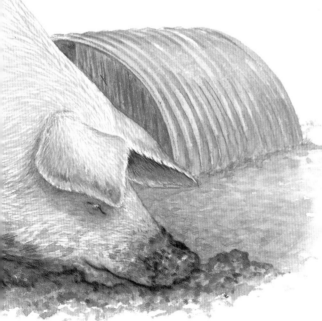

I dig up tasty roots
and worms with my
snout. This makes
me very muddy!

Here is my back.

I'm a big, heavy animal. If I roll over near you, be sure to move out of the way!

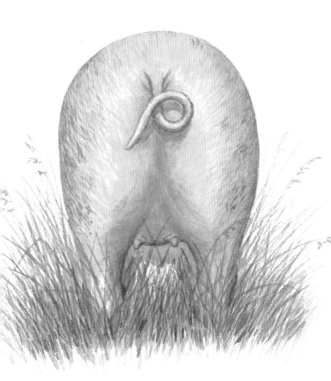

My tail is small and curly. When I run I can straighten it out so that it sticks right up in the air.

Here is my skin.

It is pink with lots
of thick, white hairs
called bristles all
over. They keep me
warm in the winter.

In warm weather
I often feel too hot.
I cool myself down
in a muddy pool
called a wallow.

Here are my ears.

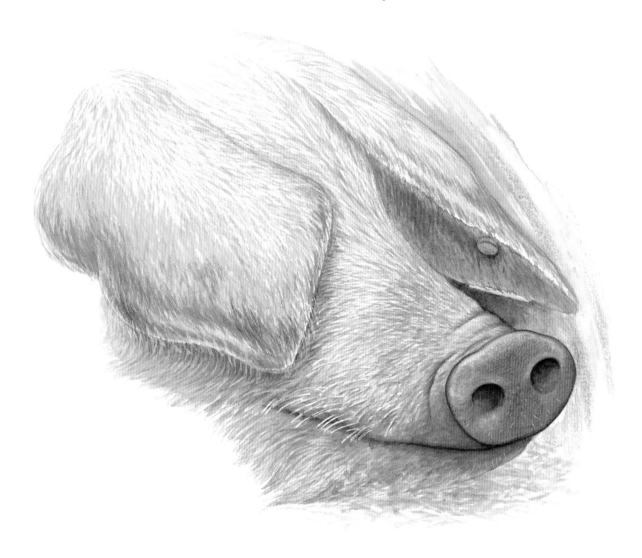

They are soft and floppy. They shade my eyes from the sun. If the weather is very hot I stay in my hut.

The farmer gives me an ear tag with a number on it. All the animals in my field have a different number.

Here is my mouth.

I have lots of teeth
for biting. I like
most kinds of food,
and I'm always
hungry and thirsty.

The farmer has put
some food in a trough.
We push and shove
to get our share.

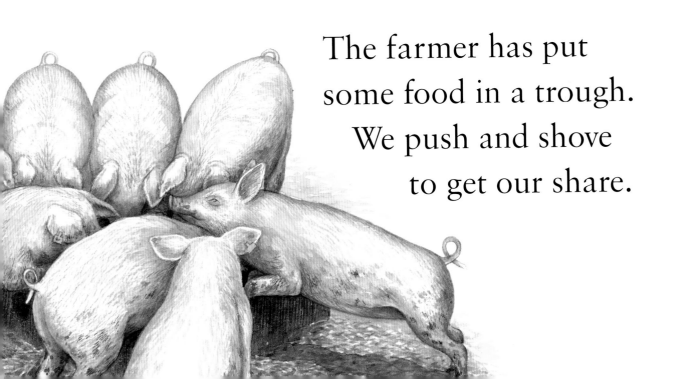

Here are my feet.

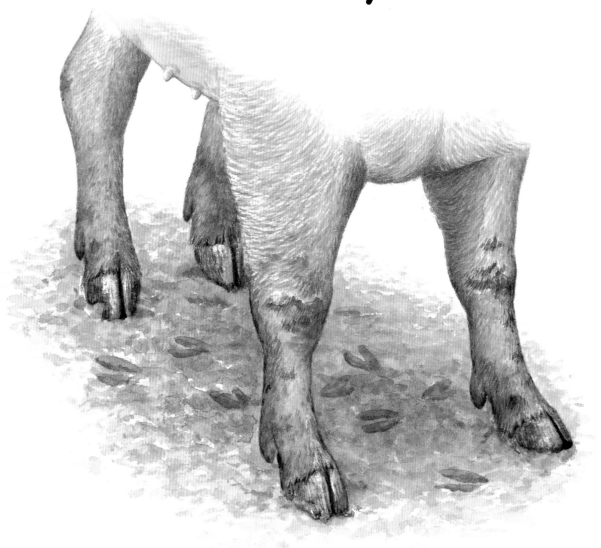

They are called trotters.
When the farmer brings
my food I run towards it.

I open my mouth and...
grunt!

Have you guessed who I am?

I am a pig.

I am called a Landrace pig.

Point to my...

curly tail

floppy ears

hairy skin   four trotters (feet)

big snout

tiny eyes

I am a sow.
A sow is
a female pig.

Here are my babies.

I have ten piglets. When they
are hungry they all squeal
at once. They drink
milk from udders
on my tummy.

As my piglets grow
they like to follow
me around the field
and play in the sun.

Here is my home.

I live on a farm with other pigs.

How many piglets can you see?
Point to a food trough, a pig hut and
the farmer busy working in the fields.

Here are some other kinds of pigs.

◄ This is an American pig called a Duroc.

► This pig is called a Saddleback. Can you guess why?

◄ Piétrain pigs from Belgium are covered in big black patches.

In some parts of the world
pigs live as wild animals
in forests. They root for food
with their long, thin snouts.

Can you answer these questions about me?

What is my skin like?

How do I cool down
in hot weather?

What are my feet called?

Do you know what
my nose is called?

What is a sow?

What are my
babies called?

Can you describe my tail?

Where do I live?

Can you name
some kinds of pigs?

Here are some words to learn about me.

bristles Thick hairs on my skin.

piglet A baby pig. Lots of baby pigs born together are called a litter.

snout The name for my large nose.

snuffle The noise I make when I am sniffing the ground for food. I grunt, too. Can you make noises like me?

sow The name for a female pig.

trotter The name for my hard foot.
I like to trot along but I can run fast, too.

trough A kind of box in the field where
a farmer puts food or water for pigs.

udder A place on a mother pig's
tummy where piglets suck milk.

wallow A muddy puddle that I like
to roll in when the weather is hot.
The mud keeps me cool.